AN INTERVIEW WITH YOUR FAMILY

THE COMPLETE GUIDE TO DOCUMENTING YOUR LOVED ONES' LIFE STORIES

BRANDON A. MUDD

BALBOA.
PRESS

A DIVISION OF HAY HOUSE

Balboa Press books may be ordered through booksellers or by contacting:

Balboa Press
A Division of Hay House
1663 Liberty Drive
Bloomington, IN 47403
www.balboapress.com
1 (877) 407-4847

Because of the dynamic nature of the Internet, any web addresses or links contained in this book may have changed since publication and may no longer be valid. The views expressed in this work are solely those of the author and do not necessarily reflect the views of the publisher, and the publisher hereby disclaims any responsibility for them.

The author of this book does not dispense medical advice or prescribe the use of any technique as a form of treatment for physical, emotional, or medical problems without the advice of a physician, either directly or indirectly. The intent of the author is only to offer information of a general nature to help you in your quest for emotional and spiritual well-being. In the event you use any of the information in this book for yourself, which is your constitutional right, the author and the publisher assume no responsibility for your actions.

Any people depicted in stock imagery provided by Thinkstock are models, and such images are being used for illustrative purposes only. Certain stock imagery © Thinkstock.

Print information available on the last page.

ISBN: 978-1-5043-3341-2 (sc)
ISBN: 978-1-5043-3343-6 (hc)
ISBN: 978-1-5043-3342-9 (e)

Library of Congress Control Number: 2015908283

Balboa Press rev. date: 10/6/2015

DEDICATION

THIS BOOK IS DEDICATED TO my father and grandfather who inspired me to capture our family stories, and to realize that this book could be a tool for everyone to use and enjoy. It is also dedicated to my wife who showed me how powerful asking questions can be at family get-togethers. It is dedicated to the generations who have already passed with their stories left untold.

May we walk in our ancestors' footsteps, passing on the family stories that illuminate and inspire our lives and the lives of generations to come.

CONTENTS

Love is experienced through the connections you make with the people you are so blessed to have in your life.

INTRODUCTION
HOW I CAME TO WRITE THIS BOOK

THANKSGIVING WEEKEND WITH MY FAMILY is usually a noisy affair. The kitchen is filled with the sounds of my mom and grandmother banging pots and pans as they prepare the turkey, stuffing, gravy, sweet potatoes and dozens of other dishes for the big dinner. From the living room comes the high-pitched scream of the referee's whistle as my father and grandfather focus intensely on televised football games. In the background, my sister and I sit tapping away on computer keyboards or pecking out text messages on our phones.

However, the Thanksgiving of 2008, I broke this family tradition to request one-on-one time with my dad to interview him about his life. And so, one afternoon that weekend, my family left the house to let me focus on him.

As I set up the camera and adjusted the lighting in the room, I could tell my dad was nervous. He was also curious about what questions I would ask. He knew I had been interviewing my maternal grandparents, but he hadn't read any of the questions I was asking them or heard any of the stories that I had been collecting. I think he also understood the significance of this interview, since his health was poor. He had been fighting cancer for over eight years. Recently, his prognosis had gotten much worse.

Now that we were finally alone together, I was frustrated with myself. Why had I waited until his health deteriorated to this point before I interviewed him? I had been home many times throughout his various treatments and had multiple opportunities to talk to him. Why hadn't I thought of it before? His disease was progressing so rapidly, I felt guilty, anxious and rushed. What if I didn't have enough time to ask all of my questions? It didn't help that I had been living in denial, refusing to come to terms with the seriousness of his illness.

For the past decade, I had kept a journal specifically for recording the stories of my maternal grandparents. From these informal interviews had grown a list of questions that I wanted to ask other family members. It almost seemed inevitable that I would interview my family one day: I had been engaging publically with people since the age of 15, when I wrote, directed, and starred in a weekly news program while still in high school. In college I had a radio show, did a stint as a mobile wedding DJ and worked for a while as a stand-up comedian. I like to engage people. Not surprisingly, my adult career is based on interviewing clients to understand their business needs.

So it felt natural for me to interview my grandparents, and it was a process I enjoyed. However, with my father, I was raising the stakes. He would be the first family member I interviewed on camera. I was excited—the visual format seemed to promise so much more immediacy than notes jotted down in a journal. My interviewing technique was taking a leap forward; my father could tell his stories in his own way. He could be himself. I was excited to think that I could go back and listen to his voice, watch his gestures, look at his face whenever I wanted.

The house was eerily quiet as we started the interview. Everyone else had gone out. There were no sounds of football games or clanking dishes. No computer screens flickered, and no phones fought for our attention. All we heard was the hum of the video camera and the creaks of the house settling. The focus was all on my dad. As I set up the camera, I was filled with love and gratitude for this moment we were sharing.

I found the perfect camera angle and locked the camera in place as he adjusted himself in the stiff chair. He needed to sit carefully, since about a month before Thanksgiving, he had had a metal rod inserted along his spine to help support his back. I knew he would struggle to be comfortable during our interview. But since he wasn't the kind of guy who would show that he was in pain, he signaled that he was ready by giving me a big smile.

I was grateful that all of the questions were prepped and ready—I could tell the interview would be emotional. I took the questions out and sat facing my ailing father. I started by asking about his childhood, realizing about halfway through that this interview might be one of the last deep conversations we would have. It might even be the only way my future children would know who their grandfather was.

Fighting back tears, I refocused on my dad. He was talking about how as a child he would wake up early every Sunday morning before the rest of his family to make himself breakfast and walk to church. Religion wasn't important to his parents and his sister, but it meant a lot to him. I also learned about how hard his parents were on his sister, and how badly he felt about that.

Two hours passed like two minutes. The rest of my family returned home just as my dad started to get tired. Our intimate conversation came to a close. We wrapped with a hug and a kiss. The time felt close and precious.

Wanting to get to know my family better had started in February of 1998. I had moved 45 minutes away from my paternal grandfather and would visit him whenever my busy schedule allowed. But since I was starting a new job, I had a lot of reasons for not visiting. He was not the kind of person who would press to see me or make me feel guilty for not coming. So excuses like being slammed at work, having house projects to finish, or women to date were completely understandable to him. They were legitimate to me, too, at the time. But I know now that if I'd really understood what was at stake, I would have made time to see him. Not only was he lonely, since my grandmother had died 11 years before, but he was a great source of stories about my own father and his childhood.

When I did manage to squeeze in a visit, my grandfather always directed the conversation towards me. He was curious about my job, my love life, and my thoughts on politics. Being a self-centered young adult, I was happy to answer his questions, missing the opportunity to ask him about himself: what were his best memories of growing up? What were his parents like? What were some of his regrets in life?

I loved his responses to my stories. His speech was sprinkled with endearing, old-fashioned expressions such as "heavens to Betsy" and "you betcha." He was stubborn and quirky, with a habit of carrying around ten dollars worth of change in his pocket. Wherever we were—at home or out at a restaurant—he would play with the coins constantly, making as much noise as a one-man band.

One day, stopping by for a visit at last, I knocked on the door but got no answer. It was strange. He was usually home alone, most of his friends having passed on. Finally, I heard him yelling. He had fallen. I didn't have a key but noticed the garage door was about six inches off the ground and somehow I squeezed myself under it. I found my grandfather in the dining room on the floor. He was hurt. Shocked, I called 911. But my grandpa yelled for me to stop. He didn't need an ambulance. He wanted my aunt to come by in the evening with her truck, load him up in the back, and then take him to the doctor.

It's hard to believe he thought this was even remotely a good idea. I spent 10 minutes negotiating with him until finally he gave in. He was tough and proud. He really needed help and he needed it right away. In fact, not only had he broken his hip, but he'd had a stroke as well.

My grandfather made it through emergency hip surgery, but he continued to have strokes. About 10 days after his fall, he passed away.

Preparing for his service, my mom, dad, sister and I spent hours thumbing through sticky picture albums trying to find some good pictures to display. We spread them across that same cool, linoleum floor that I remembered playing various games on during my childhood visits. In those faded pictures I saw someone quite different from the old man shuffling across the room with a pocket full of change. In one, my grandfather stood tall and proud next to my grandma on the day when they bought their house. In another he was dressed up to host a formal party in their home, and in another he is holding up a Manhattan cocktail with a big grin on his face. There were many of him bowling (with a tie on!). I couldn't recall ever seeing him that happy.

My dad filled in some of the stories behind the pictures, but even he didn't know everything. My grandfather had been an FBI agent in the 60s and 70s. Had he ever fired his gun on the job? I wondered. And what had inspired him to be an FBI agent in the first place? Apparently my grandparents had been serious about bowling. They frequently threw parties that lasted late into the night. My grandparents, it seemed, were quite the socialites. Yet what I understood about my grandfather was that he was strict about his kids getting good grades in school.

It surprised me to realize that we had spent so much of our lives with our families and yet we didn't really know most of the stories about them. I was upset to lose my grandfather but also frustrated that so many of his stories had disappeared with him.

I didn't want this to happen again. My maternal grandparents lived in Michigan, and when I approached them, they were more than willing to talk to me about their lives. So, I arranged to visit. I asked my grandpa about growing up around the farm. He told me how he and his brother got into trouble for ordering beer from the drug store he worked at to be delivered to barn parties they would throw, and for putting metal slugs into gumball machines. From an early age, my grandpa mowed lawns or cleaned out barns to make extra money. That entrepreneurial spirit led him to open a restaurant and then his own garage building business that my aunt and uncle still operate today. He talked about eating so much chicken during the Great Depression that he still won't eat chicken to this day.

My grandmother described being a stewardess in the 40s, and meeting her first husband—a pilot—at work. Once she married him she couldn't work at the airline anymore: company policy. Every night I would write down these stories in my journal so they wouldn't be lost.

Learning about my grandparents' lives made me feel more connected to them, and also improved our relationship. My grandfather's eyes still light up whenever I start asking questions. And hearing these stories also makes me feel more connected to everyone in my family—my uncles, aunts, cousins—as I understand more and more about where we all come from. I have a curiosity and a fascination now that I have never known before.

In fact, the more questions I asked, the hungrier I was for more details. It got so that even when I wasn't with my family, I would be collecting questions. I wanted to be ready for the next visit. And new questions occurred to me all the time. If I asked about what my grandparents' grandparents were like, I might forget to ask what they did for a living. Or, I might ask about their first job, but then forget to ask how they spent their money. I had to keep notes so that I'd remember what I wanted to ask.

And even after 10 years of interviewing them, I still worry about missing out on stories between our visits.

After my paternal grandfather passed, I was so consumed with documenting my grandparents that I hadn't realized I was overlooking some other very important people in my family. It hadn't occurred to me that anyone closer to me in age was in danger of passing out of my life soon. It wasn't until my dad got really sick that I thought about interviewing him.

In 2001, doctors found a cancerous spot on my dad's arm. A simple surgery removed the melanoma from his arm, leaving him with nothing more than a scar to remind him he had cancer. For a couple of years, all of his tests continued to be negative so there was nothing for the family to worry about. However, in 2003, they once again found melanoma on his skin. This time it was on his head. Once again he had a simple surgery and all of the cancerous cells were removed, and once again he had years of negative tests keeping the family concern at low levels. In mid-2005, my dad retired from the bench as a superior court judge. Eight months later, doctors found melanoma once again. This time, however, it was considered Stage IV: it was on one of his lungs.

After a successful surgery, my father was once again deemed cancer free so the family could take another deep breath. My dad decided not to wait for the cancer to come back this time, so as a preventative measure he did chemotherapy during the summer of 2006. Unfortunately, by the middle of 2007, the cancer had spread to his vertebrae. Further chemotherapy coupled with radiation was not easy treatment. But I never once felt that he wasn't going to get through it, just like he had done every other time.

Just before our 2008 Thanksgiving interview, my mom called me. Through tears, she explained that dad's cancer had metastasized. In fact, it had spread all over his body, including up and down his spine, making the diagnosis far more frightening.

Only at this point did I finally begin to accept the reality of his diagnosis. It didn't make sense that he could die yet.

He came home from his spinal surgery about two weeks before Thanksgiving and after that, his health began to deteriorate rapidly. He was not able to join Christmas festivities six weeks later, and just before New Year's, he entered the hospital. He went into hospice not long after that. He was on a lot of pain medication that fogged up his mind. He struggled to recall people, events, and details. I knew that I wouldn't have the opportunity to record him on camera again. After our interview at Thanksgiving, I asked him questions when I could, but at that point I was mostly just grateful to be around him.

The hospice staff supported and guided us through the difficult time, answering our questions about what to expect during my dad's transition. One hospice counselor asked my family to do an exercise together. My mom, sister, wife and I surrounded my dad. The counselor then asked us what dad meant to us and what were we going to miss about him, filming our responses. I cried harder answering that question than I did on the day my dad actually passed. How much time I'd wasted not telling him all the things I felt in my heart! How many things I'd never be able to ask him now, to know about him, and cherish about his life.

It was this moment that convinced me I needed to write this book. It wasn't just my own family that needed to get to know its members and appreciate them before they were gone, I realized. Unless everyone understands that time is truly fleeting, we will miss these precious opportunities to connect with those closest to us.

Everyone's family could benefit from spending time together in active conversation. Why wait until a mother or a father, a sister, brother, aunt or uncle is in hospice care, like I did? Why regret what you didn't say or didn't ask? Although my father and I had loved each other—as my grandfather and I had, too—we had spent more time alone with each other hidden behind newspapers, TV shows, books, Sudoku games, Facebook, etc. than talking to each other about our lives. Unfortunately, that is something I can no longer change. The good news is that the stories he did share with me are mine forever. They belong to my whole family, even to the kids I plan to have. The big thing, as I learned, is not to wait.

With this book, I have developed an easy step-by-step guide based on questions that I've asked my family—or intend to ask them. It is designed for everyone to use, even kids. The questions can be used to suit your particular needs and circumstances, whether they are more fun or more formal. And if your experience is anything like mine, you will be amazed by what you don't know—and grateful that you have the chance to ask.

Not all families are the same, and that's a beautiful thing!

Every family culture is different. How we were raised influences who we are today. We can't change how we grew up, but we can take the time to understand where we came from, and how our family members became who they are today. This book can help you cultivate a deeper understanding of your parents, grandparents, sisters, brothers, aunts, uncles and significant others. It may also help you spend more quality time with your family members and learn from their biggest life lessons.

Family dynamics change as children grow up, parents age, and people move for school, work, or love. So it is not uncommon for families to grow apart. With hundreds or even thousands of miles between family members, visits can become short, infrequent, and rushed. That is why maximizing the time you do have with your family is extremely important.

And, even if there isn't physical distance between family members, there can still be separation between them. It's common to chat about the weather or a favorite sports team or TV show, skipping right over other important things. While small talk helps us connect on a day-to-day level, when life is over, what will we remember? The weather, or how someone decided to live his life? Will it really matter how well a family member's favorite sports team did, or how the city is going down the drain? No. We want to understand people as individuals—the person who has the passion for that sports team. We want to know why they are so passionate about that team. It is time to get to know the people that we are blessed to have in our lives.

The good news is, this book will help you to ask personal questions that open up the possibility of more fulfilling relationships with not only your family members, but your close friends too. It will give you an excuse to change the next family gathering or friend get-a-way into a fun learning experience, just by following some easy instructions.

For example, you will have the opportunity to talk to a family member about a popular family dish he is making—by asking who first made it, who makes it now, where it came from and what are some key stories around this meal. Once you've collected all of these insights, the recipe will have a little extra special spice every time you make it.

And if you choose to videotape a family member making it, you will be able to pass it down in a very meaningful way. Instead of just saying, *this was a dish your great grandmother used to make*, you can actually watch your uncle making your grandmother's dish while listening to his stories about his own mother and childhood.

In the formal interview section, you can ask fun questions, such as *what was your favorite pastime when you were a kid?* But you will also have the opportunity to ask questions which are not as easy to ask or answer, such as, *What are some of the tougher challenges you have been through?* Or, *What are your biggest regrets in life?* These more difficult questions add a deeper layer to your understanding of your family. With the book, you have the perfect excuse for asking.

The questions are easy to follow and yield fascinating results. In fact, asking questions helps your family to reveal all the surprising, ordinary, beautiful, tragic, exciting, motivating, loving, and inspiring stories they have to share. It opens the door to worlds that you might have known nothing about. And the stories just keep coming.

Get ready to laugh, cry and be surprised. Enjoy the process of asking and enjoy the process of listening. These memories are a gift for you and for future generations to enjoy. Now you have the key to unlock these amazing treasures.

PART I
BEFORE YOU BEGIN

*Life's road may be bumpy, but it is the bumps
that keep the road interesting.*

CHAPTER 1

INTERVIEWING IS EASY

WE ASK PEOPLE QUESTIONS ALL the time. We ask our kids questions about school or their art projects. We ask our significant other about her job promotion or his goals in life. We ask our grandparents about historical events. We ask someone we are dating about what she does in her spare time or what interests him.

So if the thought of interviewing your family seems as foreign to you as learning Greek, don't worry. You are already interviewing people all of the time.

In fact, interviewing someone can be so natural that often it isn't even planned. For instance, I was taking a tour of an old train station in the fall of 2013 with my grandpa when he started telling stories about growing up around that station. Knowing this was a precious moment, I pulled out my cell phone and hit the voice memo record button. To keep the conversation going—and to make sure I captured the entire story—I asked simple follow up questions just after my grandfather finished speaking, such as, "That is such a fun story, do you have any more stories that you can remember?" One of the easiest ways to keep the stories flowing is to follow up each story with, "Tell me more about that ..." and include a piece of the story that was just told.

Then, before I left the station that day, I took lots of pictures. I knew I would want to make a collage of them to accompany the recording. Later, I created a memento of the afternoon. I downloaded the audio file to iMovie (an Apple application on my Mac) and added a collage of the photos I took.

To make the video even more compelling, I added other pictures I found online that illustrated the things my grandfather was talking about. For example, he mentioned that as a boy he would go to look at trains that had crashed or jumped the track, so I went online and found some pictures of vintage trains that had overturned. Then he told another story about collecting old metal slugs that he put in a gumball machine. I found some images of these and added them to the video. The project took about four hours but it was time well invested. The video turned out to be something that my family loves to watch over and over again.

Great stories get told during casual conversations all the time. They can be captured—or lost—within minutes. In many cases, you don't even need to ask a question—you just need to be present. In fact, the biggest skill you need to interview someone is recognizing a great story and trying to capture it as quickly as possible.

At one of my last family gatherings, I decided to set up a camera in the shade next to the outdoor patio table, where my family was sitting. I asked a couple of questions to get some stories flowing. To my delight, people's curiosity took over very quickly and the entire table started asking questions of each other.

This led to a wonderful afternoon of stories and reflections about how we all grew up. Nobody at that table was a professional interviewer, but we all loved to share—and when we were given the right circumstances, we all knew the right questions to ask.

It is natural to think ahead about what questions you want to ask next, or to anticipate what your family member is going to say. That can be an important part of planning. But interviewing is also about being present in the moment and actively listening to the person you are interviewing. That's where the magic happens—in the unplanned moments. With a supplied list of questions, like the ones I offer here, you can relax. The next questions are taken care of. When I interviewed my dad while he was ill, for example, having a list of prepared questions allowed me to focus completely on him and our time together. It allowed me to be present, even in an emotional moment.

This book will help you get the conversation started. It was my previous experience interviewing my family that allowed me to know what to ask at my family gathering, and to think ahead to set up the camera. But not to worry—here I share my experience with setting up an environment that makes people feel comfortable. I give you all the questions you need to start (at least, as a jumping off point—feel free to add on and keep going!), suggest where to begin, and give you tips on how to help put people at ease. So, all you have to do is follow the directions here—as if you were following a recipe. Anyone can use this book—even kids can be natural interviewers!

It is common for the person you are interviewing to be curious about how you would answer the same questions, so feel free to pass the book around. Let your grandparents, friends, partners and other family members interview you, too. This book is a tool to be shared and enjoyed by everyone.

Sniff more and bark less.

CHAPTER 2

HOW TO USE THIS BOOK

THERE ARE TWO WAYS TO use this book: by asking the questions in no particular order to spark conversation at a family get-together or social gathering with friends, or by formally interviewing family members (or close friends) one-on-one. I encourage you to use this book both ways. I have found this leads to stronger and more enriching relationships.

Before you do either of these, however, it's best to go through the entire book and read through the different types of interviews and the many different questions I've provided. Simply mark the sections and questions that are the most the most interesting to you so that you can go back and find them quickly. You might also tag the pages with sticky notes so that you can turn to them easily.

I've provided extra space at the end of most sections for additional questions you might think of. They might come to you while you're reading through the book, or right before an interview, or even after an interview when you realize there's something more you want to know. Don't hesitate to record them and use them later!

In fact, my goal with this book is not to try and provide every possible question, but to give you a starting point for deeper conversations. To help encourage the continuation of your interviews with your loved ones and share the questions you have found most fruitful, I encourage you to email me the questions with some of your stories so I can include them in future updates of this book. In this way, *An Interview With Your Family* becomes a living project that—with your help—keeps changing and growing.

Whether you are using the book formally or informally there are different tools you can use to record the stories you are hearing.

Possible Documentation Devices

- Video Camera – for formal or informal interviews and capturing stories during family gatherings.
- Smart Phone – for capturing spontaneous stories and other informal interviews.
- Digital Recorder – for formal interviews with family members who might be not be comfortable in front of a video camera.
- Journal – for taking notes to remember details of some of the stories being told by a loved one.

Video Camera

Using a video camera is great for both formal and informal interviews. In an informal situation, you can set up a camera in the corner of the room to capture the stories that are taking place. In many formal interviews, you will use a video camera to record your family member one-on-one. In both cases, it can be very helpful to have a tripod or stand so that the camera doesn't shake during the recording.

Both types of interviews require a lot of videotape or disc space. The quality of the video camera is not that important. As long as it is reliable, with clear audio and video, it is a fine camera to use for this purpose.

Smart Phone

A smart phone works well for spontaneous recordings, often in informal situations. You never know when a loved one is going to share a meaningful moment, so when he or she starts a family story, don't hesitate to pull out your smart phone and start recording. I recommend using just audio to record in these situations, so as not to distract the person telling the story. As well, video can take up a lot of room on your phone, and may cause you to run out of memory quickly. That is why I try to use a video camera for formal or casual interviews that I know will be longer than a few minutes.

Digital Audio Recorder

A digital audio recorder is great for formal interviews with loved ones who might be a little camera shy. You will still capture the passion behind their stories and they will be comfortable enough to open up. I have used the Olympus Digital Voice Recorder VN-7000 and would recommend it as an easy-to-use option. Even the most technically challenged people I know have had an easy time using this device.

Journal

A journal is great for jotting down notes as the stories are being told. When I first started interviewing my grandparents, I would usually spend thirty minutes afterwards quickly writing down all the important details. With this method, however, I could never remember everything. My suggestion is to use a journal only when a recording device is not available, or to jot down any of the names, places of interest and other specifics of the stories you are recording on video and want to remember later. Be sure to take notes as soon as possible so that you don't forget the important facts.

How to Use the Book Informally

Using the questions in this book during casual family and friend gatherings can help you get comfortable starting conversations (*see* especially Chapter 6, pages 75-87). You can ask questions that will spark engaging discussions on subjects that you may not know the answers to. You will have fun finding out!

To make finding what questions to ask easier, I have organized the questions by different types of family gatherings and different overarching categories. For instance, there is a section specifically about Thanksgiving that can be used during the next gathering for that holiday. There are also questions for non-holiday events that can be used anytime you and your loved ones gather. Additionally, you can document family recipes to preserve favorite dishes for posterity. The questions in the "Fun questions for informal gatherings" or "Three is the magic number" are perfect not only for family gatherings, but friend gatherings as well.

You may or may not want to record these more casual conversations. For example, at a large dinner party with friends and family, I would suggest just asking questions from the Family Gathering section (see Page 59) and enjoying how the discussion unfolds without recording it. In a larger party, it is harder to capture everyone's answers without running around the room with the camera—which is very distracting.

However, if you are casually sharing stories with just your family—or a small group of friends who you consider your family—I would suggest setting up a video camera in the corner of the room or pulling out a smart phone to record the conversation. These casual conversations produce some fantastic stories that you will want to have documented for everyone to enjoy later.

A great way to get an informal interview started is to take a trip down memory lane. During my family's last holiday gathering, we brought out a video montage of my grandparents' lives. My uncle had put pictures from various stages of their lives to music to celebrate both of them turning 90. Going through the video with my 90 year old grandparents sparked a long night of stories and questions that lead to a fun opportunity to learn more about our family history. My grandfather was delighted tell the story behind one of the pictures where he was sitting in a goat cart (yes, I meant to say "goat") that and his brother built for the Livingston County fair. My grandmother also added a great story about working for United Airlines, based on the picture of her in her late 1930's stewardess uniform on the steps of the plane she worked on. We all decided it would be fun to watch the video for a second time that same night, allowing us to ask about other pictures inside the video montage. We had a memorable evening being entertained with family history and stories. It sure beat watching TV!

If you decide to take this collective trip down memory lane, it will most likely spark further stories and further details about your family history. Don't forget to set up a video camera or have an audio recording device ready to capture these additional stories and details. The night we reviewed my grandparents' 90th birthday celebration, I got so caught up in the stories I forgot to pull out my phone or quickly set up my video camera. This made me realize that it is important to have devices easily accessible just in case an informal interview should start to happen. I definitely don't want to miss out on another opportunity like that one.

Quick Tips For Using This Book at Your Next Family Gathering

- Highlight and mark questions you are curious to know the answers to before the family gathering.
- Bring a physical copy of the book with you as your excuse or ice breaker to ask questions.
- Set up a camera on a tripod in the corner of the room just in case an informal interview starts to occur. Or, have an audio recording device ready.
- Set up a camera on a counter-top tripod on a kitchen counter if you are documenting a family recipe.

Informal Group Interviews

Group interviews are great because everyone can be involved. The interview can become part of the special time together, whether it's a holiday, vacation, family reunion or Sunday dinner. At a recent family gathering for the holidays, I set up a camera in the corner of the room to capture everyone decorating a Christmas tree. Then I started asking them questions about what the holidays were like for them. Everyone took turns talking about toys they remember receiving, gifts they gave and funny stories around the holidays. It was also interesting to hear a story from different perspectives when two people give the narrative of the event.

So if you intend to use this book at your next family (or friend) gathering, I encourage you to highlight all of the questions you want to ask beforehand. What are some you don't know the answers to? That way, since you won't be doing structured interviews with people, you will be prepared when the opportunity to ask questions presents itself. For example, the question, "What was your favorite gift that you received growing up?" is a great place to start at a holiday gathering with your family, as well as, "Was there something that you always wanted but didn't get?" Have these prepared ahead of time. You may be surprised by what you learn!

I also suggest making the interview process fun—even joking about some of the questions. This helps to set everyone at ease. You might open with something like, "Hey, I just read this interesting book that had all these questions in it to ask family members. I actually didn't know a lot of the answers so I thought it would be fun to ask everyone a couple. Would you mind?" That easy question could be a doorway to fascinating new stories about your loved ones.

Once your group interview is done, download it from your camera, audio recorder, or smart phone to another place such as your computer, a thumb drive, or a back-up drive for safe-keeping. Label it with the date and a basic description of the content. For instance "Childhood stories, family reunion 4/19/2015," or in the last example, "Christmas stories, whole family December, 27, 2013."

From here, you can either leave the video as it is and upload it to a free online service such as You Tube or Drop Box, where family members can access it, or you can take a couple of hours to edit out all of the pauses and lulls in the conversation, add a title screen that says who was in the film and the date the conversation took place, and any pictures that help to illustrate the stories that were told. Then, upload the edited content for family members to access at their leisure. (For more information about saving, editing, and sharing material, *see* Chapter 2.)

How to Use the Book for Formal Interviews

The other way to use this book is to conduct formal interviews with your loved ones either with audio or video (*see* especially Chapter 4, pages 37-57). This may include chronicling the stages in a child's life, too. The formal interview sets aside uninterrupted time to completely focus on a loved one. It requires a little more work: you will need to plan when and where to conduct the interview, and prepare a comfortable space for your subject. But nothing expresses how much you care about someone more than making time to focus exclusively on them and their story.

And luckily, capturing your loved one's story has never been easier. We are fortunate to live in a time where we have access to many inexpensive recording devices and video cameras. And I provide lots of questions to get you started and keep the interview going (coming up in Chapter 5, pages 58-74).

Documenting your loved one will help you to remember the details of stories they've told over and over again. How many times have we tried to tell a family story we had heard "a million times" only to find that we could not do it with the same passion or flair that our family member did? When you capture these stories for good, you will have access to all the details forever.

Video recordings are the ideal way to allow future generations to see their relatives' physical expressions as they talk. However, cameras automatically make the interview process more formal and can make people nervous and shy. Think about how it feels to pose for a photo (self-conscious) versus having someone spontaneously snap your picture before you have time to think (more natural).

Convincing your subject to participate may become easier once you explain that you don't want to lose the fantastic stories they have told in the past—or that you want to get to know the stories of their lives better. You might remind them how much fun it is to thumb through sticky photo albums—often ones they spent so much time and care assembling. Then ask them to envision what it would be like if those photos could talk! We want to be able to hear—in their own words—what is important to them.

Still, it's also true that some people will not want to be recorded on camera. Audio recordings are perfect to use with family members who have a harder time opening up. Audio still captures a loved one's stories in their own words, while conveying the passion behind their stories, too. The downside of this type of recording is that you won't be able to see your loved one's expressions or gestures as they talk. However, you can add in a visual element later by editing in a photo collage of your family member that will play along with the audio recording.

Once a loved one has agreed to an interview, you will want to get ready for them, setting the scene for the most successful interview possible. Making plans ahead of time to put your family members at ease will increase your chances of creating a comfortable environment in which people feel relaxed and unselfconscious.

Prepare for the formal interview

1. Plan a specific time to interview your loved one. Set the date/time and remind them of the event when the day and hour get closer.
2. Scout out the best location to conduct the interview.
3. Buy twice the amount of videotape or memory cards as you think you need for the interview (more on this in Chapter 3, page 22).

4. Test the recording device(s) the day before the interview *(see* Chapter 3, page 23*).*

5. Let your enthusiasm for your interviews show! It's contagious and will help to get your subjects excited, too.

6. Create a loving, fun, open environment that your loved one feels comfortable in.

7. Provide snacks, beverages and tissues within easy reach of the person being interviewed.

8. Set the expectations of the interview—tell them that you will take breaks and that they can skip questions if they don't want to answer them.

9. Have a clock behind the person you are interviewing so that you can see it and keep track of time.

10. Understand basic camera angles, shots and how to light the room for the best effect (more on this in Chapter 3, page 23 & 24).

11. Start each interview by stating who you are interviewing, the date (including the year) and location where the interview is taking place.

12. Start the recording while the interview is being setup. Your subject might start telling stories even before you're ready. Keep the tape rolling during breaks to be sure to catch off-handed remarks that might later become treasures.

Plan the time

It's true that without making concrete plans, things never seem to get done. Therefore, the first thing to do in more formal interviews is to call your loved one, explain the idea of interviewing them, and set a day, time, and place to meet.

Then try to pick a meeting time when there is nothing else going on. Even though a family holiday seems like a natural first choice—since everyone will be together in one place—these occasions can also be distracting. Your family member may prefer to go back to the festivities rather than answer your questions! So whether at a family gathering or during a less hectic visit, find a time when your subject won't feel rushed or pulled away from the moment.

In preparation for the one-on-one interview, consider sending your subject a couple of the questions beforehand. Give them time to think of some stories in advance. It will also give them an opportunity to see your excitement at interviewing them, and perhaps make them less shy about participating.

Scout out the best location to conduct the interview

It is important to choose a location where you won't be interrupted and where disruptive noises will be kept to a minimum. Specifically, try to avoid areas near noisy heaters or air conditioners. However, do make sure the temperature is kept at a moderate level or perhaps on the cooler side which helps keep the subject's energy level up.

Let your enthusiasm for your interviews show

Interviewing your family members should be a fun and rewarding experience for you as well. Let your excitement about documenting your family show when you invite people to be interviewed. Family and friends will pick up on your enthusiasm and will have a harder time saying no to you.

Create a loving, fun, and relaxed environment where your loved one feels comfortable

People will only open up to the point that they feel comfortable. The more comfortable the environment is, the more they will open up with their stories. Your goal is not to interrogate them or create a family Watergate, just establish a loving environment to let them tell their story.

You can do a lot to help nurture a comfortable environment by staying patient, calm, and curious. Since you intend to ask thought-provoking questions about things your loved ones probably haven't thought about in years, it is important to give them time to reflect. It's fine to have moments of silence. Give them the space to recall their stories before they respond. If you rush to move on to the next question, you might lose the magic.

It is your job to make sure the process of being interviewed isn't intimidating for your subject. Try lightening the mood with funny—but appropriate—comments, such as:

- "You know how hard it is for me to remember things—that's really why I need to record you."
- "I may not be [pick one: Barbara Walters / Bob Woodward / Oprah / Chris Beck / Larry King / Jon Stewart], but it is about time that someone interviewed you about your amazing story!"
- "Don't worry about the camera, it is one of the new models that takes off 20 pounds!"

Have your goal be making your subject feel comfortable.

Provide snacks, beverages and tissues

To make your subject feel comfortable, it's helpful to provide snacks, tissues, water and maybe an adult beverage nearby so that your subject doesn't have to get up or change the flow of the conversation.

Ask ahead of time what their favorite snacks are and have them on hand at the time of the interview. You can say things like,

- "As a thank you for giving me the exclusive interview, I want to have a couple of your favorite snacks ready for you. What would you like to eat or drink?"
- "We all know every major celebrity or rockstar has a green room filled with all of their favorite snacks so I don't see why the rockstar in my life shouldn't have them, too. Please let me know what you'd like!"

You can always say this in your own way, as long as you mean what you say.

Tissues are always helpful to have within easy reach for the unexpectedly emotional moments. Trust me on this one.

Set expectations

Before you ask the first question, it is important to set expectations with the person you are interviewing. Explain why the interview is so important, how long it will last, and what will happen to the recording after you are done. Here is a list of helpful things to tell your interviewee:

- that you will be asking a lot of questions and that it is okay if there are some they don't feel like answering.

- that this interview is not just for you but for many generations to come. You are doing it out of love for them and love for the family.
- that you want to get to know the stories of their lives better.
- that you want to get to know your whole family better.
- that since we now have a way to pass down family stories so future generations can know their ancestors better, you are making the effort to record them for posterity. Their story is a part of that.
- that there will be regular breaks about every hour or so, depending on how the interview is going. However, if they need a break sooner for any reason, it's fine to ask.
- that you will be compiling the results of your interview and sharing them. Let your subject know what you plan to do with this material, and when they can expect a copy (or how you plan to share it).

Remember, the goal is to make them feel comfortable. The more comfortable they are, the deeper they will go into their stories.

Have a clock visible behind the person you are interviewing —and take breaks

It is important to have a clock behind the person you are interviewing. You will need to have some way to check the time without your subject noticing. You don't want them to get distracted by wondering how much time has passed.

This is important for two reasons.

First, some cameras have a limited recording time available. You want to avoid asking a question if the answer could get cut off.

Secondly, you will want to take breaks. Breaks help to keep your subject comfortable. A break about every hour or hour-and-a-half is a good rule of thumb. However, if someone is sharing a lot of great stories, wait until it feels natural to take a break.

After someone has told a very intense story, you can check in by simply asking, "how are you doing?" or "can I get you anything or could you use a break?" You don't want your subject to feel uncomfortable and they may not think to ask for a break themselves.

However, do not turn off the camera during these breaks—except to change tapes/disks. The stories that happen during breaks are just as important as the ones told during the interview.

Take all the time you need for the interview. Enjoy the stories and embrace the time to be present with your loved one. Feel free to cry, hug and joke with them, if that feels natural. If the moment gets really emotional, put down the book, turn off the camera if you need to and just be present. Showing your love and concern is more important than moving on to the next question.

Start each interview the same way

To properly document the interview, start by stating who you are interviewing, the date (including the year), and where you are conducting the interview. This simple statement will help you organize your videos as you compile multiple interviews.

Keep the camera rolling

Start the recording while the interview is being setup so that if your subject starts telling stories before you're ready, you won't miss them. Along these lines, keep the tape rolling during breaks to catch off-handed remarks that might later become treasures.

The questions in Part 2 of this book are organized into different moments in people's lives, so you just have to go directly to the area of interest that you want to ask about in the interview.

Just like a snowflake, every family member is different. Remember and record this beauty of uniqueness for future generations to enjoy.

CHAPTER 3

RECORD, PRESERVE, AND SHARE YOUR MEMORIES

To conduct a successful interview, you will need to have working recording equipment, ways to edit the material, preserve it, and share it. Documenting an interview does require a little extra time but the results will last for generations to come. It is a small price to pay for a gift that will be enjoyed by so many.

Buy enough videotape or memory cards

One of the easiest mistakes you can make is not buying enough videotape or memory cards for your video or audio device. As the interview starts to flow, time will also start to fly by. The last thing you will want to do is cut off someone halfway through an emotional story to attend to a technical issue. It will ruin the flow of the interview and may hold your subject back once the recording starts again.

As a simple rule, plan on doubling the number of tapes or amount of memory you think you will need to document the interview. It is not uncommon to have to change the tape after only asking 5-10 questions.

Great Apps to have on your Smartphone

- Voice Memos comes on the iPhone. Other smartphones will have similar apps.
- Audio Memos Free – Voice Recorder. This app was designed for longer audio files.
- Voice Record Pro – Simple and easy to use.
- Voice Recorder (free) – This app allows you to organize your recordings and even includes a way to add them to your Drop Box account.
- Garage Band – Great for editing your voice recordings to take out unwanted silent moments.

Test the recording device

Electronics fail all the time. And they often have a tendency to fail at the worst possible times. Testing the recording device the day before your interview will help reduce the potential electronic meltdown at the crucial moment. I also suggest having a backup device on hand in case your main one shuts down. That way, you won't lose the time with your family member trying to resolve a technical difficulty.

Basic camera shots and angles

Knowing some basic camera shots and angles is very helpful for conducting interviews. You are not trying to win an Emmy, but you also want your recording efforts to be the best they can be!

A few examples and tips:

Wide Shot: The camera is pulled back so the entire person and a large part of the environment the person is standing or sitting in are shown. This shot is a great shot to be used for any group interviews.

Medium (Mid) Shot: The camera shows the person from about the waist up but still includes a large part of the environment that they are standing or sitting in.

Medium Close Up: The camera is filled with just the person's body from about the waist up. There is very little environment, as the person is the main focus.

There are two important things to do when filming your interviews. First, leave a lot of room in the shot so the family member can move to take a drink of water or shift in their seat freely without moving out of frame. Since you will be setting the camera shot and then sitting down in front of them to ask the questions, you don't want to be worried about them jumping out of the frame of the camera. That is why the ideal shot for a formal interview is a Medium (Mid) Shot (as seen in image 2). It is close enough to see your loved one's facial expressions but gives them space to move and adjust without worrying about them being cut off in the camera shot.

For another option, two cameras can be used to not only create a video backup but it will help give your interview two different visual perspectives that can be edited together to highlight specific moments in the video for better viewing engagement. It is still important to leave as much room as possible so a loved one can move around. A Medium Close up shot (as seen in image 3) is as close as the camera should get. Any closer and a loved one could easily shift in their seat and out of frame for the rest of the interview.

Second, it is not necessary to include yourself in the camera shot. Even though it is typical to see news organizations use an over the shoulder camera angle showing the back of the interviewer's head and shoulders, this particular interview is about the family member or friend, not the person conducting the interview. Also, it's not as interesting to watch someone looking at their notes. It takes away from the person being interviewed. The only exception is during group interviews where the entire room of friends or family should be captured. For all group interviews, a wide shot should be used to capture as many people as you can.

That being said, since the microphone on the camera will be behind you when you are conducting the formal interview, it is important to state your questions clearly and loud enough for the camera to pick them up. Your audience should be able to hear what you asked, as well as how the subject answered. Depending on the room in which you are conducting the interview, you may want to consider buying a microphone that you can connect to your camera and place in between you and your loved one(s) to make sure all of the audio is captured.

Once you have finished the formal interview, the person you are interviewing may be curious about how you would answer the same questions. This is an opportunity to then be a part of the filming during the formal interview —but only then.

Lighting

Following a few simple rules of thumb can make lighting an interview straightforward and effective. The first thing to remember is to not point the camera directly into a light-filled window, otherwise your subject will appear in silhouette on the tape. Instead, situate the person you are interviewing so that light is coming towards him or her from the side, not from behind or directly in front of them. This will help limit the amount of shadowing on the person's face.

Second, before you begin, record about 20 seconds of video and then play it back for yourself. Confirm that the lighting works the way you want. Once you are happy with the clarity of the person you are interviewing and have limited the amount of shadows, you are usually ready to start.

Those two steps are really all you need to know as far as lighting is concerned. However, if you want to learn about more lighting techniques, you can find lots of free advice online by searching Google or YouTube for "lighting techniques for a TV interview" or "lighting techniques for film."

Use a Tri-Pod—or Not

Use a tri-pod whenever possible to keep your camera shots steady for any recording lasting more than a couple of minutes. If a tri-pod is not an option, one of the best ways to steady your camera is to hold your arm with your free hand. This will steady the camera shot and support your arm so that it doesn't get tired as easily. However, if a tri-pod is not used, you will need to make sure that your questions are laid out on a table or chair so you can reference them while using the camera.

When recording how a family recipe is made, consider using a tabletop or collapsible tri-pod to help steady the camera in tight areas like a kitchen. Just place the camera on the tabletop tri-pod at the edge of the counter top near the person cooking. However, make sure the camera is not too far out of your reach. You want to be able to grab the camera to get a close up of a specific measurement, should the moment present itself.

Preserve Your Material

Once you have recorded your interview, you will want to back it up. It's very easy to misplace your audio or video documentation. Imagine taping over priceless footage of Dad's 60th birthday, or spilling coffee on an audio tape recording of Aunt Mabel singing her favorite childhood songs. Not a good thing.

During the chaotic time when my dad was passing, I lost the main footage of our first interview. To think that prized treasure might be gone forever is a terrible feeling. No one should have to experience anything similar.

So, immediately following an interview, take the time to save everything in a digital file. I recommend saving it to up to three separate back-up drives and keeping them in different locations. If you lose one copy, then you still have more available. One copy should be on your main computer, and two can be on other drives such as memory sticks (USB drives) or external hard drives or online cloud storage. I now keep my interviews on one USB drive that I store at work and another one I store in a fire-proof safe at home, in addition to the one saved on my computer.

Make sure you label them in an easy to remember way such as "Family Interviews 2014," so you can find them at a later date.

In addition to backing files up on a computer, you may also want (or prefer) to back the video files up on online cloud storage or websites that store video files. For online cloud storage, trustworthy companies such as Carbonite, Mozy, Sugar Sync, I-drive, Norton or I-backup can help back everything up for a monthly fee. The benefit to using these services is that you don't have to worry about your hard drive dying or your hardware being lost or stolen. The downside is that they are not free. As well, you may have to remember passwords and, in worst case scenarios, the information could become vulnerable.

The bottom line is to back everything up and remember to continue to back up as you record more interviews. Also remember to back up while you are editing the video or audio, if you choose to do that. Save the main video first and make multiple copies that can be stored in different locations. As you edit footage, or add in music or still photos, be sure to save new copies with each version. Think of the main raw interview file as any other important computer document that you need to handle carefully.

Review the Material to Ask More Questions

Once the video is backed up, the next step is to review the interview. Take notes on what follow up questions you might ask next time or what questions you missed. Sometimes a loved one will spend an hour on one question. When you review the tape, you may realize they still didn't answer some important questions. I always think of great follow up questions after the interview, things that I should have asked to learn more about. I write them down so that I'm ready to start the next interview with those specific questions.

Asking follow up questions about a specific story your loved one told in the first interview helps to show them that you were really listening to them, and are interested in them and knowing the complete story.

The second reason to review your footage is to give you a reason to request more time with a loved one. For example, instead of just requesting another interview you can say, "We spent an enjoyable afternoon talking about your childhood but I have more questions about what it was like raising children that I would love to learn more about, could we schedule some more time together?" Being specific with your request will set a goal for the next interview and will give your loved one an understanding of the direction the interview will be going.

Edit Your Material

Sometimes just having the raw videos themselves is reward enough. However, once you've completed your interview and properly backed it up, you might consider editing the video footage into a movie. Or, you might create a video from an audio recording by adding photos that relate to the stories being told. Editing can also help take out unnecessary material and add in more visual context. This is an optional step, but the results are well worth the effort.

The big benefit to editing your footage is that it allows you to take out all the extra pauses, coughs, sneezes, and downtime when not much is happening in the video or audio recording.

It also allows you to skip ahead to the good stories when your subject is rambling.

As well, editing the video or audio recording allows you the option to add photos to go along with the stories. This is my favorite editing tip. Adding pictures makes a video pop and helps to bring the story to life. Adding more visual context will make the movie easier for future generations to understand and enjoy.

Most of the time you will only need to do very basic editing. The editing software available these days is very easy to use, so the editing process need not require much time. You will need to transfer the video footage to your computer and upload it into the editing program. Several good programs are available such as Sony Movie Studio, VideoStudio, Windows Live Movie Maker and iMovie (my preference is iMovie). If any of your friends have done amateur video editing, I suggest asking them which program they like, too.

Share Your Material

Once you've finished an interview, downloaded it, labeled it, and maybe edited it, you will need a way to share it with your friends and family. You can post and share files right away with such services as YouTube, DropBox, and Google Drive.

You can either request that the people sign up for a free account—that will give them access to all the digital files, notes and pictures you post there—or, if they are not comfortable online, you can send them a direct link to the material.

Saving a file on Dropbox

1. Open a free account at www.dropbox.com.
2. Upload your videos, pictures and notes to your account.
3. Under "Share a Folder," set up a new folder to be shared. Name it "Family Memories" or something that you can easily remember.
4. It will ask you to invite members to that folder. Type in your family members' email addresses. They will now have access to that folder.

Saving a file on Google Drive

1. Open a free account with Google at www.google.com.
2. Download the Google Drive folder to your computer.
3. Upload your video to your account by either dragging the file into the folder or saving it directly to the folder.

YouTube

YouTube is different than Dropbox or Google Drive. It is a much more public option but it does have a privacy layer so you can control who has access to your videos.

The best way I have found to keep my videos private, but also give my family access, is to mark the videos "unlisted" and place them in a dedicated "playlist" that you set up. You can do this in the video manager section on your YouTube channel. Then open up the playlist with your videos and send your loved ones a link to that folder.

It is important to note, however, that YouTube will only allow you to upload videos of up to 15 minutes long. Personally, I don't mind breaking up my interviews into 15-minute segments because it can be easier for family and friends to enjoy shorter episodes. To help organize the videos I label them by part. For example, "2015 Family Interview, Dad Part 1."

The biggest benefit to sharing your videos on YouTube is, once they are uploaded to the website, they are completely backed up. They become much harder to accidentally delete.

Saving a file on You-Tube

1. Open a free account at www.youtube.com.
2. Upload your video to your account.
3. Under "Basic Info" of your video, click the arrow next to the box that says "Public." A dropdown list will appear. Click on the word "Unlisted."
4. Next, click on the "Playlist" button listed under "Video Manager."
5. Click on "New Playlist." Title it something like "Family Playlist."
6. Next, open up your video manager that lists all of your videos you have uploaded. Put a checkmark next to the family videos then click on the "Playlist" dropdown to add them to your "Family Playlist."
7. Open your "Family Playlist" and then copy the link to share with your family and friends.

With Dropbox or Google Drive, you can save and share pictures, documents, and other files in different formats. However, you can only save a certain amount for free. After that, you will need to pay a monthly service charge.

Other options for storing larger files are Humyo, File Dropper, Sizeable Send, WeTransfer, Glide's gDrive, Send This File, DivShare, Box.net, Streamfile, Dropio, Gigasize, Mailbigfile, youSendit and Sendspace. Some of these are free services and some require a small fee.

If you are not comfortable with technology, just know that there is always help close by. In your Google search (go to www.google.com), simply type in the question you are having challenges with, such as "how do I create a DropBox account?" and then click the "enter" button. You will find some helpful answers quickly. If you prefer to have someone walk you through your questions, you can type in the same question (such as "how do I create a DropBox account?") in the search bar at YouTube to find a video of someone explaining the answer.

Other Ways to Share

If posting family stories online is not something that you feel comfortable doing, here are a couple of other suggestions I have for sharing your family video treasures.

Dinner and a movie with your loved one: Invite the loved one you interviewed to watch the video with you. Make them dinner and toast the fact that their story is preserved for future generations to enjoy. This could spark more stories that you may also want to record. It will also help them understand the importance of documenting their story and may encourage other family members to participate in the process.

Family movie premiere night: Create a movie premiere night that celebrates the family stories you have captured. Invite the family over, pop popcorn, offer champagne and sparkling cider, pass out appetizers, or plan a family potluck to help create a celebration. Use this as an opportunity to get more of the family members to participate in the interview process.

Feature the movie at the next family gathering: Show the recording at the next holiday gathering, family reunion, or get-together. After you show the recording, pass a copy of it out to everyone in attendance and request time with any family members that haven't been interviewed.

Be sure to get the consent of the loved ones whose interviews you will screen. Only when they've given their permission should you begin to plan the party or screening. You may want to explain the importance of getting other members participating in the process and how having the party could help with that.

PART 2
CONDUCTING THE INTERVIEWS

*Every book is a quotation; and every house is a
quotation out of all forests, and mines, and stone quarries;
and every man is a quotation from all his ancestors.*
—**Ralph Waldo Emerson**

CHAPTER 4

THE FORMAL INTERVIEW WITH FRIENDS AND FAMILY

LIGHTS, CAMERA, ACTION! ARE YOU ready to begin? The chapters in Part 2 are filled with thought provoking questions to get the interviews started—and keep them going.

There are a lot of questions in each of the following sections of the book, but don't worry—you don't need to get through all of the questions in one sitting. Flag the ones that seem the most important, then take your time and enjoy the stories your subject is telling.

Then, relax. If you are anxious or frustrated, the person you are interviewing may speed up their stories or be less willing to talk. You might miss out on some of the details and magic of what they are telling you.

There is no way to mess this up so relax and enjoy the process!

Using the checklist below, take a moment to review how to set up the formal interview (covered in Chapter 2, pages 6–21 and Chapter 3, pages 22–34). Make sure you don't miss anything before you begin!

Checklist: Preparing for a Formal Interview

- o Set up a specific time and date with the family member.
- o Share your excitement about the interview.
- o Find a private and quiet location to conduct the interview.
- o Have extra videotape and/or memory cards as backup.
- o Test the recording device the day before the interview.
- o Create a fun, relaxed environment.
- o Have snacks, beverages, and tissues handy.
- o Let your family member know what to expect (including the expected length of the interview).
- o Place a clock behind the person you are interviewing.
- o Remember to take breaks.
- o Light your subject from both sides and don't shoot directly into an open window.
- o Leave extra room in the camera shot.
- o Start each interview by stating your loved one's name, location and the current date.
- o Have fun!

Tips for Conducting Formal Interviews

The formal interview is one of the best ways to show a family member that you care about them: you are dedicating time and energy to learning his or her story. Here are some things to keep in mind—and practice with every interview:

Remember to listen

Ask your questions, and then listen to the answers. It can be one of the hardest things to do. But people truly appreciate an interested listener. It will help them to open up.

Ask for clarification

Ask for clarification even if you think you don't need it. You can use phrases like, "tell me more" or "what was that like?" or "what did you think about that?" to get deeper into your subject's thoughts.

Don't interrupt

If your subject is involved in a story, but you have a question, wait until they finish before asking it. Write it down so that you don't interrupt the flow of the story and remember to ask it later.

Ask follow-up questions

When you interview, remember to pause after every question to give your subject enough time to reflect and answer in their own way. Also, be sure to ask follow-up questions to help your subject elaborate. Here are a few examples:

- Tell me more about that time you just mentioned when …
- What else was going on during that time?
- Do you have any more memories of that period of your life?
- How would you describe that time?

Asking these kinds of questions gives people permission to go a little deeper into their stories. It also shows that you are engaged and interested—which helps people to relax, too.

Even if you only get to ask a couple of questions, starting the dialogue will open up the possibility of deeper conversations in the future. Listen closely and have fun.

Be present

Watch for signs that your family member is tiring. Don't push them to continue if they are showing signs of being done. It is much easier to start again later when he or she is feeling up to it.

If you push the interview, your subject's answers may become shorter and less complete. It's usually better to thank him or her for participating, tell them what a great job they did, and set up a time to continue the conversation.

Use props and family heirlooms

Before you interview a loved one, make copies of old pictures, pull aside some unique family heirlooms (jewelry, hats, special family items, etc.) and have them ready to reference during the interview.

Expect the unexpected

No matter how much a person prepares for an interview, there can still be technical difficulties. Instead of getting frustrated with the camera, or any other recording device, simply have a basic pad of paper ready to conduct the interview. Time that is set aside to interview a loved one is precious, so I suggest not losing that time even if it can't be recorded.

Set up a time for a follow-up interview

If it makes sense, schedule a time for another interview. Let you subject see your enthusiasm for the project and your desire to record their complete story.

Checklist: Conducting a Formal Interview

o   Remember to listen.
o   Ask for clarification.
o   Don't interrupt.
o   Ask follow-up questions.
o   Be present.
o   Use props and family heirlooms.
o   Expect the unexpected.
o   Set up a time for another interview.

Quick Interviews (Short Formal Interviews)

If time is tight, or if you're having trouble choosing what questions to ask your subject, use the quick interview list I've supplied. This grab-and-go version is highlighted in a box below (page 42) and includes key questions about each part of people's lives. And then if you end up having extra time, you can go back to a particular moment you want to learn more about and ask more questions about it.

Even though the quick interview contains fewer questions, that doesn't necessarily mean it is going to be fast. Depending on who you are interviewing, your subject could spend over half an hour giving detailed answers for each question. Let them talk and try not to think about the time. You can always ask them to do a second interview. You might even say at the beginning, "if we don't get through all of the questions, would it be alright to schedule another interview?"

The quick interview may leave out questions you feel are essential to ask, so feel free to customize the question list however it works best for you and your interviewee.

Quick Tips for Asking Questions

1. Highlight the questions in the book that you want to ask. Consider flagging the pages with sticky notes, too, so that you can find the questions easily.
2. Use pictures or family heirlooms as props for the interviewee to remember their stories more clearly.
3. Stay calm and don't rush to get through all of the questions.
4. Ask follow-up questions instead of immediately going to the next question on the list.
5. Write down any new questions the book missed on the lines provided.

Quick Interview: Short Question List
(choose 2 from each section)

Start the interview by stating the interviewee's name, age, the date and say where the interview is taking place.

KIDS WILL BE KIDS (childhood)
- Describe what your family was like growing up: What was your Dad like? Mom? Brothers? Sisters?
- What are some of your favorite memories growing up with your brothers and/or sisters?

- What were your siblings like as kids?
- How would you describe yourself as a kid? What were your favorite activities growing up?
- What are your favorite memories of your grandparents? Great grandparents? Aunts? Uncles? What were they like?
- How would you describe yourself as a student? (Class clown, jock, popular, outsider, etc.)
- What was the proudest moment of your childhood?

YOU HAVE TO GROW UP SOMETIME (college & early adulthood)

- What did you do when you graduated from high school?
- What was your favorite part of the career/job path that you chose? (If your subject has had multiple jobs or careers ask them to tell you their favorites from each one.)
- If you could go back in time would you choose the same profession? Why or why not?
- (Family loss) What age did you lose your mom? Dad? How did you handle that? What do you miss most about them?

LOVE HAPPENS (falling in love and forming partnerships)

- How did you meet your wife, husband or life partner?
- Describe one of your favorite dates. Where did you go, what did you do? What car were you driving? What were you wearing? What was s/he wearing? What music was playing?

- What words of wisdom would you share with future generations about how to make a marriage/relationship work?

FAMILY MATTERS (having a family)

- How did you decide to have kids—or not to have kids?
- How did pregnancy change things in your marriage?
- Describe how you felt as a new parent.
- What were some of the biggest lessons you learned raising kids?

LIFE KEEPS MOVING ON (reflecting on the big picture)

- What are the biggest life lessons you have learned?
- What would you like your grandkids and their kids (and their kids!) to know about you?
- Looking back on your life, what were your favorite memories?
- Looking forward, what memories would you like to make?
- In what ways are you like your dad or mom? In what ways are you different?
- In what ways are you like your siblings? In what ways are you different?
- How do you envision your funeral? Are there specific things you would want or don't want at your service?
- Is there anything you have always wanted to do that would include me that you haven't done? Let's put that on the calendar and do that within the year. (Make plans to do it.)

Interview With Your Family: Full Question List

Start the interview by stating the interviewee's name, age, the date and where the interview is taking place.

KIDS WILL BE KIDS (childhood)

<u>Family</u>
- Where were you born?
- Describe what your family was like growing up. Dad? Mom? Brothers? Sisters?
- What was it like growing up in your household? Describe your daily chores. What was a typical day like? Week?
- Describe your dad.
- Describe your mom.
- Describe the house you grew up in. What did it look like? How was it set up? (If your subject lived in more than one house, have them describe each one.)
- What memories do you have from growing up in that house? (Or, their favorite house)
- What was your relationship like with your brothers and sisters? What are some of your favorite memories growing up with them? What were they like as kids?
- What are your favorite memories of your grandparents? Great grandparents? What were they like?
- How would you describe your aunts and uncles? Did you have a favorite?
- What are some of your favorite memories with other family members (e.g. cousins/godparents)?
- Do you remember any stories of their childhoods?
- Did you go on an annual vacation(s) with your family when you were a child? What was it like? Where did you normally go?

- Did you take a family vacation that you can remember that you really enjoyed? Why did you pick that one?
- Describe your parents during your childhood. What were they like? What interests did they have? What is your favorite memory of that time?

<u>Holidays & Celebrations</u>
- What was your favorite memory of Christmas/Hanukkah/ Kwanzaa?
- What was a typical Christmas/Hanukkah/Kwanzaa like in your family?
- What was a typical Thanksgiving like in your family?
- What was your favorite Thanksgiving memory?
- Describe any family holiday traditions that you experienced growing up.
- Did your family do anything special for New Year's Eve?
- How did your family celebrate other holiday's like ...
  o Martin Luther King Day
  o President's Day
  o Valentine's Day
  o Veteran's Day
  o Memorial Day
  o Fourth of July
  o Labor Day
  o Father's Day
  o Mother's Day
  o Easter
- What was your favorite birthday memory?
- What is your favorite kind of cake/candy/ice cream?
- What was your favorite gift growing up?

School

- Describe your elementary and middle schools growing up. Do you have any memories of a specific teacher who made an impression on you? Do you remember their names? (If your subject brings up high school, let them continue to give you all the information you can get.)
- What were your favorite subjects?
- Were you ever suspended from school?
- How would you describe yourself in elementary school or middle school?
- How would you describe yourself in high school?
- What were your grades like growing up?
- How would you describe yourself as a student? (Class clown, jock, popular, outsider, etc.)
- What was high school like?
- Did you ever get in trouble? What did you do? How often did you get in trouble?

Hobbies & Pastimes

- What sports did you play growing up? Which one was your favorite? What are some good stories or fun memories of playing that sport?
- Was there one sport or activity that you were particularly good at? Did you win any trophies or awards for your accomplishments?
- What were your favorite activities growing up?
- Did you ever collect things growing up (e.g. stamps, stickers, baseball cards, dolls, pez dispensers, etc.)?
- What activities did you do most with your friends?
- Were there any games you liked to play?
- How did you spend your summers growing up? What activities do you remember doing over a typical summer?
- What did a typical weekend look like growing up?
- What were some of your favorite "hang out" spots with your friends?

Growing Up

- How would you describe yourself as a kid?
- Who were you "best friends" with as a child? What were some of your favorite memories of spending time with this person?
- What is your favorite childhood memory?
- What were your family's thoughts about religion? What religion, if any, were you raised in?
- Did you have a favorite book when you were young?
- What was your favorite toy growing up?
- What was the one toy/thing you wanted as a kid, but never got?
- What did you wear at that time (what was the style)?
- Have you ever broken a limb? Which one(s) and how?
- What was your favorite kind of music growing up? Who were your favorite artists?
- Did you attend any concerts? Which concerts were your favorites? Is there a band/artist you wish you could see today?
- What was your favorite food growing up? How about your favorite meal?
- Did you have any pets? What were their names and what type of animals were they?
- What did you want to be when you grew up?
- How were you punished when you did something bad? Were you ever spanked?
- Did your parents approve of the friends you had?
- Did your folks ever tell you that you couldn't date someone? Why did they forbid you to see them?
- Did you ever have a pen pal? Who were they? Where did they live? How long did you write each other?
- What was the biggest national event that you can remember? How did that event affect you? Were there any other national events that stick out in your mind that really affected you?

- What was the saddest event you can remember in your childhood?
- What was the happiest event you can remember in your childhood?
- What was the name of your first girlfriend or boyfriend? How old were you? Do you remember any funny stories?
- What was your most embarrassing moment as a kid? How about as an adult?
- How did your family approach the conversation about sex and where babies came from?
- Was sex discussed openly in your family?
- What was the proudest moment of your childhood?
- What was your favorite movie as a kid?
- Do you have any memories of going to the movies? What was it like? How much was a ticket, etc.?
- Did you have a job as a kid? What was your first "real" job? Second? Third? Describe what you did for each job and if you liked the job or not.
- What was your favorite job growing up? Describe one of your favorite memories of that job.
- What would you spend your money on?
- What was your first major purchase that you made with your own money as a child?
- Do you have any childhood regrets?
- OTHER QUESTIONS TO ASK

_____

_____

_____

_____

_____

_____

<u>YOU HAVE TO GROW UP SOMETIME</u> (college & early adulthood)

<u>College and/or living on your own:</u>
- What did you do when you graduated high school?
- Did you go to college? Was that an expectation in your family?
- If you didn't go to college, do you regret not going?
- Did you lose contact with your friends from High School after graduation?
- Is there someone you wish you had contact with today? Why them?

If your subject went to college:
- What college did you go to?
- How did you decide on that college?
- What did you study?
- Did you change majors or did you keep the same one throughout college?
- What was your favorite class?
- How well did you do in college?
- What activities/groups were you involved in?
- Were you involved in a sorority or a fraternity?
- Describe the friends you hung out with in college.
- What was your favorite college memory?
- What was your biggest accomplishment?
- What was your biggest learning experience during your college years?
- How would you describe yourself in college?

If your subject went away for college or left home after high school:
- Describe the first house or apartment you lived in.
- What memories do you have of that first place?
- How did you feel moving away for the first time?
- What was your favorite memory of that time?

o   What did you miss most about living at home?

o   What did you enjoy most about living on your own?

o   What were some of the challenges you faced living on your own for the first time?

- What was the biggest life lesson you learned in the first year after leaving your parent's home?

Sex

o   What were your thoughts on sex at this point in your life?

o   When did you lose your virginity?

o   Was sex everything you thought it would be?

o   Was there anything that someone could have explained to you that would have made your first time more enjoyable?

o   Do you think it would have been better if you had waited?

- Did you feel that you were prepared to live in the "real world?"

- What were your thoughts on politics at this stage in your life?

- What were your thoughts and opinions on religion?

- (If your family member/friend is really feeling comfortable) What was your parent's stance on drugs and alcohol? When did you have your first drink? Did you ever use drugs?

- (Family loss) What age did you lose your grandparents? How did you handle that? What do you miss most about them? What did you learn from them?

- (Family loss) What age did you lose your mom or dad? How did you handle that? What do you miss most about them? What did you learn from them?

Entering the Workforce

- After high school or college, what did you want to do for a job/career?
- Did you have trouble getting your first job in the area you wanted?
- What was your favorite part of the career/job path that you chose? (If your subject had multiple jobs or careers ask them to tell you their favorites from each one.)
- What was your biggest work or career accomplishment?
- What was your biggest work or career lesson?
- If you could go back in time, would you choose the same profession? Why or why not?
- Do you have any regrets from this time?
- OTHER QUESTIONS TO ASK

_____

_____

_____

_____

_____

_____

LOVE HAPPENS (falling in love and forming partnerships)

- How did you meet your wife, husband or life partner?
- What is your favorite memory of her or him?
- Do you have a song that is/was special to you both?
- When did you know he or she was "the one?"
- Did you ever do anything embarrassing while dating? What was it?

- Did he or she ever do anything embarrassing while dating you? What was it?
- Describe one of your favorite dates. Where did you go, what did you do? What car were you driving? What were you wearing? What was he or she wearing? What music was playing?
- What was your first impression of her or his parents? Did you get along with them?
- Describe the proposal. Who asked whom? Were the parents asked first? How did they react? How did you feel about the proposal?
- Where did you go on your honeymoon?
- What were some of the traits that attracted you to her or him? Why did you choose this person?
- What were the first years of marriage like?
- What did you learn?
- Describe the first house you lived in.
- What were some of your favorite memories of those first couple of years?
- Did you ever cook for him or her? What did you make? Do you still cook for him or her?
- All relationships have ups and downs. What were the most challenging times for your marriage? How did you get through it?
- What has been the best time of your marriage so far?
- (If there was a divorce) What did you learn most from going through a divorce? Why do you think the marriage didn't work out?
- What happened with your first wife/husband/partner? Do you have any regrets from that marriage? If you could help someone else going through a divorce, what advice would you give him or her?
- What was the best vacation you ever took with your wife/husband/partner?

- What words of wisdom would you share with future generations on how to make a marriage or relationship work?
- OTHER QUESTIONS TO ASK

_____

_____

_____

_____

_____

_____

FAMILY MATTERS (having a family)

- How did you decide to have kids —or not to have kids? What was that like?
- How many years were you married before you had kids?
- How did the pregnancy change things in your marriage?
- (For men) How would you describe your wife/partner as a pregnant woman? Did she crave anything funny?
- (For women) How would you describe each of your pregnancies?
- How would you describe the birth of your first child? How did your feelings change with the second/third/etc.?
- What was your favorite memory of the first year of raising your first child?
- Describe how you felt as a new parent. Were you anxious? Happy? Depressed? Contented? Did that change?
- What are your favorite memories raising children?
- What was your favorite memory of me as a kid (if applicable)?
- What were some of your biggest challenges raising kids?

- Did you have a favorite book about raising kids?
- What advice did you get when you were raising kids? Who gave you that advice? Would you pass any of that advice on to a parent today?
- Did you have a baby shower? What memories do you have of the shower? Did you have a shower for each baby?
- Do you remember the day your child first went to school? What was that like?
- Do you have any funny stories of raising kids? Do you have any funny stories about me?
- Do you remember what foods your children liked? How about the ones they didn't?
- If you were to describe each child in one word, what would it be and why?
- What were some of the biggest lessons you learned raising kids?
- After being a kid, and then having kids, did you have any preconceived ideas of what your kid's childhood should be? Was it different than what you imagined?
- How did having kids change your marriage?
- As your kids grew into adults, how did that change your life?
- OTHER QUESTIONS TO ASK

_____

_____

_____

_____

_____

_____

LIFE KEEPS MOVING ON (reflecting on the big picture)

- What is one accomplishment that you are really proud of?
- Who was a mentor in your life?
- Who were the major influences in your life?
- What are some things that you haven't done yet that you want to experience?
- Name some places that you haven't visited yet that you would like to.
- What are some things that you want to accomplish that you haven't completed yet?
- What is one thing that, 30 years ago, you would have had no idea would be true today?
- What is one thing you miss from 30 years ago?
- In what ways are you like your dad and mom? In what ways are you different?
- In what ways are you like your siblings? In what ways are you different?
- Describe your ideal day.
- What was the proudest moment of your life?
- What are the biggest life lessons you have learned?
- What has been the hardest part of your life and how did you overcome it?
- Looking back on your life, what were your favorite memories?
- Looking forward on your life, what memories do you want to make?
- What is the best place (country, city, state) you have ever visited? What did you enjoy there? What food did you enjoy?
- How would you like to be remembered?

- How do you envision your funeral? Are there specific things you would want or don't want at your services?
- Is there anything you have always wanted to do that would include me that you haven't done? Let's put that on the calendar and do that within the year. (Make plans to do it.)
- What would you like your grandkids and their kids (and their kids!) to know about you?
- What words of advice would you pass along to your grandkids and their kids and so on?
- OTHER QUESTIONS TO ASK

_____

_____

_____

_____

_____

_____

Everyone carries some baggage; just make sure it fits in your overhead bin.

CHAPTER 5

QUESTIONS FOR INFORMAL GATHERINGS

GATHERINGS OF FRIENDS AND FAMILY make great occasions for informal discussions—and great storytelling. As I mentioned in Chapter 2, you may decide not to film an informal gathering so that guests feel free to open up without fear of a recording ending up in a public space. However, if your group is willing, set up a camera in the corner of the room to record the interactions. People tend to be more relaxed in group settings and less concerned about a still camera, especially if it is out of sight. A camera on a tripod in the corner of the room is much less intrusive than holding the camera or a smart phone up to capture a special moment. This set-up allows you to be able to capture some candid answers and exchanges.

Before the event, review the questions you want to ask. Or, have the book with you for quick reference. Of course, not all of the questions will be appropriate, so choose the ones that fit the occasion.

During a recent New Year's Eve celebration I attended with friends, we went around the table and asked some of the questions listed in the New Year's Eve section below. Even though I was there with friends I knew well, I was surprised by some of their answers. When asked about their resolutions, people gave expected answers, like losing weight and finding a new job, but one close friend surprised me by saying that he wanted to become a father. It was a good reminder of how important it is to spend quality time with loved ones—and ask them about what's meaningful in their lives.

Finally, these gatherings usually involve one key ingredient: food! This section ends with suggestions for how to record and document your friends or family members making favorite dishes so that you can preserve—and enjoy—all of your favorite people making their most delicious food.

Quick Tips for Recording Family or Friend Gatherings

- Use a tri-pod, whenever possible, if you plan to set up a camera.
- Place the camera out of the way in the corner of the room so people forget they're being recorded.
- If you don't have access to a camera, or if people spontaneously start telling great stories, use your smartphone or digital recorder to capture the stories.

Fun Questions for Informal Gatherings

- Using only one word, describe everyone in this room.
- What's your most embarrassing moment? What's the most embarrassing thing you have witnessed another person doing?

- What are some things you got in trouble for doing during your childhood?
- If you had all the money in the world, what would you want to accomplish during your lifetime?
- If money were no object, what would your perfect date be?
- Did you ever play hooky from school? What did you do? Did you get caught?
- Who has been your favorite president and why?
- If you were to describe high school in one word, what would it be? Why?
- If you were to describe your childhood in one word, what would it be? Why?
- If money were not a factor, what would be your perfect day? Who would you spend it with? Where would you go? Would the day change if you had to do it alone?
- When was the last time you felt completely happy? What were you doing? Who was involved with that memory? Why did you choose that moment?
- As a child, what did you do for fun?
- When did you have your first boyfriend/girlfriend? Who was it? What memories do you have of being with that person? Are you still in touch with them?
- As a kid, what did you always think you were going to be when you grew up?
- How did your family approach the topic of sex with you growing up? Which parent took the lead? What did they say?
- Did any girls in your high school get pregnant? How did people react to that?
- How old were you when you had your first alcoholic beverage? What was your favorite drink back then? How about now?
- If you had to be an animal, which animal would you be and why?

- What is the best advice you have ever received?
- What do you like most about yourself?
- What big challenge have you taken on recently?
- Who's the most famous person you have ever met?
- What's the most memorable TV commercial you have seen?
- Do you believe in life on other planets?
- What is something you have done that surprised you?
- What is your favorite holiday and why?
- Do you believe people are better off now or 50 years ago? Why?
- What do you think is the greatest invention of all time? Why?
- What do you believe is the secret to a long life?
- What is the wildest thing you have ever done?
- What do you think is the secret to a successful marriage?
- What concerns you most about the future?
- Do you have any superstitions?
- Do you believe in ghosts?
- What has been the best decision of your life (marrying your significant other doesn't count)?
- What was one of the most frightening moments in your life?
- Describe one of the happiest moments when you were a child. How old were you? What were you doing?
- Were you ever teased or bullied as a child? What happened?
- What is one new thing that you have learned in the last week?
- What was the first movie you can remember seeing in the theater?
- If you could be invisible for a day, what would you do?
- How have your priorities changed over time?
- What is the most unusual thing that has happened to you while on vacation?
- If you could wake up tomorrow with the ability to play a new instrument, which one would you choose?

- What does "success" mean to you?
- What was your favorite TV show growing up as a kid?
- What is your least favorite chore that you have to do? Why?
- If you could pass on one piece of advice for future generations, what would that be?
- If you could ask your future self a question, what would you say?
- If you could go back to your high school self, what advice would you give?
- Do you believe men or women have it easier in our culture? Why?
- If you could change anything about your childhood, what would you change?
- Describe a perfect evening for you.
- If you were a superhero, what powers would you have?
- If you chose a movie title to represent the story of your life, which movie title would you pick?
- What do you plan on doing in retirement?
- What do you dream about?
- If you had a time machine, where would you go and what decade would you like to be in? Why?
- If you could change one thing about yourself what would you change? Why?
- If you were stranded on an island and you could only pick one item from each of the following categories, what would you choose?
  - Tool
  - Book
  - Movie
  - Album/Musician
  - Food item
  - Person to keep you company
  - Board game
  - Musical Instrument

o   Alcoholic beverage
o   Non-alcoholic beverage
- If you could ask God one question, what would you ask?
- Describe your life in one word.
- Have you ever been in a physical fight? Who was it with and what was it about?
- Have you ever had a spiritual experience? What happened?
- What is your religious background?
- Did your parents argue a lot when you were a kid? What did they argue about?
- When you were growing up, whom did you go to for advice?
- OTHER QUESTIONS TO ASK

_____

_____

_____

_____

_____

_____

Three is the Magic Number

Unlike the previous questions, the following ones require shorter answers. They dive into a person's priorities, as well as how they rank things. The questions are in no particular order so have fun, skip around, and enjoy learning something new about your loved ones.

- Name 3 things you like about each person in this room.
- Name 3 things you want to accomplish in the next year.
- Name your top 3 vacations.
- Name 3 places you still want to travel to.

- Name 3 celebrities (dead or alive) you wish you could have dinner with.
- Name 3 celebrities (dead or alive) you never want to have dinner with.
- Name 3 of the best meals you have ever had.
- Name 3 of the best concerts you ever attended.
- Name your top 3 movies of all time.
- Name your top 3 books of all time.
- Name your top 3 bands of all time.
- Name the 3 best qualities about yourself.
- Name 3 things you would like to change about yourself.
- Name 3 things that make you smile.
- Name 3 people whom you wouldn't mind passing the time with at the DMV.
- Name 3 things you admire about your mom.
- Name 3 things you admire about your dad.
- Name 3 traits you look for in a significant other.
- Name 3 wishes you would ask for if a genie came out of a bottle to grant them to you.
- Name 3 traits you look for in a friend.
- Name 3 boyfriends/girlfriends from your youth. What do you remember about them?
- Name 3 of your biggest accomplishments.
- Name 3 people you admire.
- If you became the president of the United States tomorrow, what 3 issues would you tackle first? How would you deal with them?
- Name 3 things that annoy you.
- Name 3 things that scare you.
- Name 3 things that you are passionate about.
- Name 3 food items you could never live without.
- Name 3 food items you dislike.
- Name 3 things you should give up this year.
- Name 3 things you should start doing this year.

- Name 3 things you still would like to do in this lifetime.
- If your house was burning and you could only save 3 items, what would you save?
- Name 3 jobs you would love to have.
- Name 3 jobs you would never do.
- Name 3 things that upset you.
- Name 3 wishes you have for your family.
- Name 3 wishes you have for your friends.
- Name 3 wishes you have for our government.
- Name 3 wishes for humanity.
- Name 3 wishes for future generations.
- Name 3 things that you are proud of the most.
- Name 3 things you like most about each one of your kids.
- Name 3 things you like about your significant other.
- Name 3 of your favorite childhood toys.
- Tell 3 funny family stories.
- Name 3 things you would do if you won the lottery.
- Name your top 3 TV shows of all time.
- Name 3 things you would never do.
- Name 3 of the most attractive people.
- Name 3 of the most sensual experiences you have had.
- Name 3 sexual fantasies you have had.
- Name 3 things you would like future generations to know about you.
- Name 3 things you would want at your funeral.
- Name 3 things you want to learn.
- Name 3 things that make you laugh.
- Name 3 things that make you cry.
- Name 3 people that have been a big inspiration to you.
- Name 3 things you are grateful for.
- Name 3 life lessons that were tough to learn.
- Name 3 of your favorite gifts you have ever received.
- Name 3 things you love to do in the winter time.
- Name 3 things you love to do in the summer time.

- Describe the top 3 scariest moments in your life.
- If you knew you were going to die within the next month, what 3 things would you do right away?
- What are 3 things we could do to have a closer relationship with our family?
- If you could go back in time, what 3 past events would you like to attend?
- OTHER QUESTIONS TO ASK

_____

_____

_____

_____

_____

Mother's Day

Questions for mothers

- What was your favorite Mother's Day? What did you do?
- Do you remember your first Mother's Day as a mom? What was it like?
- If you were to give advice to future mothers, what would you tell them?
- What has been the biggest lesson you've learned as a mom?
- How would you celebrate Mother's Day growing up as a child?
- What are some of your favorite memories of your mother?
- If you were to pass along your wisdom to a future father, what advice would you give on how to best support a woman during her pregnancy?

- If you were to do it all over again, would you have raised your children any differently?
- How would you describe your pregnancy (or pregnancies)?
- What was one strange thing you craved while being pregnant?
- What was the thing that scared you the most about being a mom?
- Did you do anything to prepare to be a mom?
- Describe one of the proudest moments you have had as a mom.
- What mistakes do you feel you made while raising your children?
- How did you feel your relationship changed with your significant other once children came into the picture?

Mother's Day general questions

- Was Mother's Day celebrated in your home? What was Mother's day like growing up?
- How was it celebrated?
- What did you typically eat on Mother's Day?
- Who did the cooking on Mother's Day?
- What special thing did you used to do on Mother's Day? How about now?
- Describe your Mother. Grandmother?
- OTHER QUESTIONS TO ASK

_____

_____

_____

_____

_____

_____

Father's Day

Questions for fathers

- How would you typically celebrate Father's Day?
- What were some of your favorite memories of your father?
- What was your favorite Father's Day? What did you do?
- Do you remember your first Father's Day as a Dad? What was it like?
- What was the thing that scared you the most about being a dad?
- Did you prepare in any way to become a father?
- If you were to give advice to future fathers, what would you tell them?
- What was the biggest lesson you learned from being a dad?
- Describe one of the proudest moments you have had as a father.
- What mistakes do you feel you made while raising your children?
- How did you feel your relationship changed with your significant other once children came into the picture?
- If you could go back in time, would you change anything about how you raised your children?

Father's Day general questions

- Was Father's Day celebrated in your home? What was Father's Day like growing up?
- How was it celebrated?
- What did you typically eat on Father's Day?
- Who did the cooking on Father's Day?
- What special thing did you used to do on Father's Day? How about now?

- Describe your Father. Grandfather?
- OTHER QUESTIONS TO ASK

_____

_____

_____

_____

_____

_____

Thanksgiving

- What were some of your family traditions around Thanksgiving?
- What are some other family traditions from past generations?
- Has there ever been a tradition you have wanted to start around Thanksgiving but never told anyone about? Describe the tradition. Why haven't you started it?
- What was typically served for dinner on Thanksgiving in your family?
- What was your happiest memory during a Thanksgiving celebration?
- What was your earliest memory of Thanksgiving?
- Was there ever a Thanksgiving that didn't go as planned? What happened?
- What are you most thankful for this last year?
- If Thanksgiving was taken away, what would you miss most about the holiday?
- OTHER QUESTIONS TO ASK

_____

_____

_____

_____

_____

_____

Christmas/Hanukkah/Kwanzaa

- What was your earliest memory of Christmas/Hanukkah/Kwanzaa?
- What was a typical Christmas/Hanukkah/Kwanzaa like in your family?
- What did you like most about Christmas/Hanukkah/Kwanzaa?
- What was the best gift you ever received?
- What were some of your family traditions for the holiday?
- If you were put in charge of starting a new tradition this year, what would you suggest doing?
- What was typically served for the big meal? What was your favorite dish? What is your least favorite dish?
- What was your favorite memory of Christmas/Hanukkah/Kwanzaa?
- Have you ever experienced a Christmas/Hanukkah/Kwanzaa celebration that didn't go as planned? What happened?
- OTHER QUESTIONS TO ASK

_____

_____

_____

_____

_____

_____

New Year's Eve

- What was something you intended on doing this year but didn't? What do you think held you back from completing it?
- What was your biggest takeaway from last year?
- What was the earliest New Year's Eve celebration you can remember? Did you stay up until midnight?
- Describe some of your favorite New Year's celebrations. What did you do? Why do those celebrations stand out over others?
- Did your family have any New Year's Eve traditions growing up? How about now?
- What was celebrating New Year's like growing up in your family?
- Describe some funny memories of past New Year's celebrations.
- What was the most exciting thing you did last year?
- What were your biggest accomplishments last year?
- What were you the most proud of last year?
- What is one thing you would like to do or accomplish in the coming year?
- What is one thing you would like to start doing, and what is something you would like to stop doing next year?
- If you were to start a new tradition around New Year's Eve, what would you suggest doing?
- OTHER QUESTIONS TO ASK

_____

_____

_____

_____

_____

_____

<u>Documenting Family Recipes</u>

Family recipes are often passed down from generation to generation. But for some reason, no matter how much we may make a favorite dish, it always seems to taste better when our original loved one made it. To help get the taste closer to what you remembered growing up, the next section will help you document your favorite recipes, as made by your relatives (or close friends).

For example, at your next family gathering, you might talk to a family member about a popular family dish he is making. You might ask who first made it, who makes it now, where it came from and what are some key stories around this meal. Once you've collected all of these insights, the recipe will have a little extra special spice every time you make it.

And if you choose to videotape a family member making it, you will be able to pass it down in a very meaningful way. Instead of just saying, *this was a dish your great grandmother used to make*, you can actually watch your grandmother making the dish while listening to her stories about her own mother and childhood.

This should be especially helpful to people whose family members usually cook from their senses verses measurement. My mother loves to tell the story about how she had to go step by step through how my great grandmother made her famous pumpkin pie. She could never get the taste correct on her own, and her grandmother had never written the recipe down. She cooked by feel. One day, my mother had her grandmother put every "pinch" of this or "spoonful" of that into measuring utensils so she could write down actual proportions of ingredients. That way she could precisely document the recipe the way she remembered it tasting as a little girl. I am really glad she did because it is one of my favorite family recipes today.

The family recipe interview is simple to do and requires just two steps. The first step is to set up a camera on a tri-pod just out of the way of all of the cooking activity but close enough to capture the necessary audio and visuals. A tabletop or a collapsible tri-pod placed on the counter is ideal for this recording. If the kitchen is not an open layout, and there is limited counter space for filming, it is fine to not use a tri-pod at all. Remember, the goal is not to create a perfect movie, but rather to capture the family recipe and the stories that go along with it.

The second step is to ask questions about the background of the recipe and learn about stories related to when the dish was made and enjoyed.

Ask questions when there is a lull in the cooking, such as when the dish goes into the oven, or when an ingredient needs to be chopped, mixed, marinated, or boiled. Just make sure not to ask questions before a loud mixer is required or the garbage disposal or dishwasher needs to be run. The loud noises may muffle the story that your loved one will tell.

Quick Tips for Documenting your Family Recipes

- Use a tri-pod whenever possible (ideally a tabletop or collapsible tri-pod).
- Place the camera out of the way but easily accessible so you can grab it for necessary close ups.
- Make sure you ask for tips on how to make this dish. Sometimes the secret to making a family recipe isn't the ingredients or the measurements but the uniqueness of how it is prepared.
- Have the interviewee state their name, give the current date (including the year) and announce what recipe they will be making.

Questions to Ask While Cooking

- Are there any tips I should know about before preparing this recipe?
- What's the secret ingredient that makes this dish so good?
- What is your first memory of eating this dish?
- When was this recipe typically made?
- How did you learn to make it? Who taught you how to make it?
- Who created the recipe? Where did it come from?
- What are your fondest memories of making the dish?
- What is your happiest memory of eating this dish?
- Who else in the family knows how to make the dish?
- Have you ever messed up making the recipe? Did someone else? What went wrong?
- Do you remember any other recipes that your family used to make but for some reason they haven't made in a long time?
- What are some of your favorite recipes?
- Did you enjoy cooking growing up?
- Who taught you how to cook?
- Do you (or did you) host a lot of dinner parties? What did you typically make for large parties?
- What was dinnertime like for you growing up?
- Are you allergic to any foods?
- Did any of your family members have dietary challenges?
- OTHER QUESTIONS TO ASK

_____

_____

_____

_____

_____

_____

*The greatest gift you can give a child is
the gift of undistracted time.*

CHAPTER 6

CHRONICLING YOUR CHILDREN'S LIVES

DOCUMENTING CHILDREN FROM THEIR OWN perspectives is a great opportunity to hear how kids think at each stage of their lives. What are they learning? How do they feel about growing up? What are their daily challenges and what are they learning from them? With all the footage parents have of their kids, they still might not know the answers to these questions.

This section includes five interviews at five major stages of growing up: preschool, elementary school, middle school, high school, and young adult. Capturing children in their own words at each stage makes the photos, artwork, and writing they are also doing, more exciting. Children—who are always fascinated by the question, "who am I?"— will love the one-on-one attention now, and be curious to review their answers as they get older. Parents and grandparents, needless to say, will be thrilled to review the results as well.

In preparation for each interview, create a safe and fun environment for a child to share his or her thoughts and feelings. Include the child in the process, letting him or her choose a quiet place where they feel most comfortable. Make an appointment with them and treat them like a grown up subject. Turn off all phones and let the other family members in the house know what is going on so they won't disturb the interview, perhaps even requesting that they do something outside the house so all of the attention can be focused on the child being interviewed. With very young children, you might want the parent present to help make the child feel comfortable. You can decide on a case-by-case basis.

The questions I've supplied change depending on how old the child is. However, some of the questions will be repeated at each stage of life. I did this deliberately so that you can capture how children's opinions change over time. Remember, not all of the questions need to be answered. Just as with your other subjects, take the time to figure out the most important questions you want to ask before you go into the interview, highlighting them or otherwise marking them in your book.

In the preschool, elementary and middle school stages you will want to limit the number of questions you ask to match kids' shorter attention spans. One way to work around this is to conduct the interview over the course of a couple of days throughout a year.

Encouraging Children to Open Up

Children are individuals with their own thoughts and feelings. Refrain from judging them just as you refrain from judging all of your subjects' thoughts and opinions. The responsibility of the interviewer is to ask the questions and listen to the answers.

As hard as it might be, it is important to not comment on children's answers. Rather, use neutral and encouraging comments such as:

- That is interesting!
- Tell me more.

- What did you think about that?
- Can you explain that further?
- I never knew that about you, please go on.
- That must have been tough, how did you get through that?

The bottom line is to keep the conversation going. Have fun! It is fine to express emotions but it is important that the focus is on the child, and to make sure that he or she feels comfortable and loved.

Kids are motivated by different things in each stage of their lives. You can try making the first interview fun by giving them a makeover, suggesting they get dressed up (or even buying them a new outfit), asking what special drink or favorite snack they would like during the interview. The more you make the interview a big deal, the more they will be into it. Let them know they are the most important celebrity in your life and you want the exclusive interview.

Interviewing Teenagers

By the time children reach adolescence (and high school), they may not only be opinionated but consumed with their own social life. It may be harder to get teenagers to unplug from their devices or be out of touch with their friends for the hour or two you need to do the interview. To have some quality one-on-one time, try to catch them during the holidays when things are quieter and boredom might have set it. Or, you might consider taking them on a day trip away from their normal routine or an overnight trip where they can completely remove themselves from life's distractions.

At this stage in their lives, most teens feel they are being judged by their peers, teachers, and society in general so it is extremely important to refrain from judging any of their answers. Treat them as adults and really listen and acknowledge their answers. They may be reluctant, but gently nudge them to tell their stories. You might tell them that they really matter to you and their story will be lost if they don't tell it.

You might also suggest to your teenager that they can interview you if they would like after you are done. Allowing them the same opportunity will help them feel less vulnerable. If you are comfortable with it, let them know that no question is off limits and the goal of the interview is to have a better understanding of each other's life story.

You can close this series of interviews by making a DVD of all of the interviews and giving it to your loved one as a gift. The process of doing this series of interviews is really the true gift to each other and this time will be extremely memorable for both parties.

Quick Tips for Interviewing Kids and Teenagers

- Make the interview a big deal. Provide kids with their favorite drinks and snacks.
- Include kids in the interview set-up process. Ask them where they would like to be interviewed to make them feel most comfortable.
- For younger kids, suggest that they get dressed up for the interview or consider giving them a makeover.
- Allow younger kids to have special toys, dolls or stuffed animals with them during the interview.
- For older kids, you might suggest going on an outing together, or even a day trip, to have more one-on-one time.
- Ask for privacy from the rest of the household family.

- Remind the child or teenager that they are the celebrity in your world and you want the exclusive interview about their lives.
- Refrain from judging kids' answers. Instead, use neutral comments as you would with adult subjects to get them to open up.
- Allow kids to interview you after your interview with them.

Interview with Preschool Kids: Question List

- Please state your name and how old you are.
- What is your favorite color?
- What is your favorite food? Snack? Meal?
- What is it like being __ years old?
- What is your favorite movie or TV show?
- How would you describe yourself?
- How would you describe your dad?
- How would you describe your mom?
- How would you describe your brother? Sister?
- What is your favorite kind of cake/candy/ice cream?
- Who are your "best friends?" How would you describe them? What are your favorite things you do with them?
- What do you want for Christmas/Hanukkah/Kwanzaa or your birthday this year?
- What is your favorite toy? Why do you like it so much?
- Have you ever been in trouble? What did you do?
- Do you have any pets? What are their names and what type of animals are they? Do you have any funny stories about them?

- What do you want to be when you grow up?
- OTHER QUESTIONS TO ASK

_____

_____

_____

_____

_____

_____

Interview with Elementary School Kids: Question List

- Please state your name and how old you are.
- What school do you go to? Where is it located?
- What is your favorite subject?
- Who is your favorite teacher?
- What is it like being ____ years old?
- How do you feel you have changed since last year (or, since last grade)?
- Tell me a funny story that happened at school.
- What has been your biggest accomplishment in school?
- What is your favorite book?
- What is your favorite movie?
- Describe your weekly chores. Do you have a favorite?
- How would you describe your dad?
- How would you describe your mom?
- What is your favorite part of Christmas/Hanukkah/ Kwanzaa?
- What is your favorite birthday memory?
- What is your favorite kind of cake/candy/ice cream?
- What has been your favorite gift you have ever received?

- What do you want for your birthday this year?
- How would you describe yourself?
- Who are your "best friends?" How would you describe them? What are some things you like to do with them?
- What toys do you enjoy playing with? Do you have a favorite toy?
- What sports do you enjoy playing? Which is your favorite? What are some good stories of playing that sport?
- What are your favorite activities/hobbies?
- What kind of music do you enjoy listening to? Who are your favorite artists?
- What is your favorite TV show?
- Have you ever been in trouble? What did you do?
- What is your favorite food? How about your favorite meal?
- Do you have any pets? What are their names and what type of animals are they?
- What do you want to be when you grow up?
- Do you have a pen pal? Who are they?
- What is the happiest event you can remember?
- What has been your favorite vacation?
- What would you like to tell your high school self (in the future) about who you are right now?
- OTHER QUESTIONS TO ASK

_____

_____

_____

_____

_____

_____

Interview with Middle School Kids: Question List

- Please state your name and how old you are.
- In one word, how would you describe yourself? Why?
- What is it like being ___ years old?
- What has it been like growing up in (year & place)?
- Describe what you do during a typical week.
- What school do you go to and what is your favorite subject? What do you like about it?
- Who is your favorite teacher? Why?
- Tell me a time when you did something really embarrassing.
- Tell me a funny story that happened over the last couple of years.
- What are you most proud of?
- What makes you happy?
- What is your favorite movie?
- Describe all of your weekly chores. Do you have a favorite?
- How would you describe your parents?
- What was a great memory of Christmas/Hanukkah/Kwanzaa?
- How would you describe Thanksgiving at your house? Do you make any special food?
- What do you want for your birthday this year?
- If you could only have one cake/candy/ice cream flavor, what would it be?
- What is one thing you love about yourself?
- Who are your "best friends?" How would you describe them? What are some things you do with them?
- Have you and your friends ever gotten into trouble? What happened? Is everything okay now?
- Tell me a secret about yourself.
- What sports do you enjoy playing? Which one is your favorite? What are some good stories or fun memories of playing that sport?

- What are your favorite activities/hobbies?
- What is your favorite TV show?
- What bands do you love listening to? What's your favorite song? Can you sing some of that song?
- If you could be anyone in the world, who would you want to be?
- What is your favorite food? How about your favorite meal?
- Do you have any new pets from the last time we had an interview? What are their names and what type of animal are they?
- What do you want to be when you grow up?
- What is the happiest event you can remember?
- What has been your favorite vacation?
- What would you like to tell your grown-up self (in the future) about who you are right now?
- OTHER QUESTIONS TO ASK

_____

_____

_____

_____

_____

_____

Interview with High School Kids: Question List

- Please state your name and how old you are.
- What is it like being ____ years old? How would you compare that to what it was like being in middle school or elementary school?
- What high school do you go to and what is your favorite subject?

83

- How would you describe what high school is like? What do you like about it? What don't you like about it?
- Who is your favorite teacher? Why is this person your favorite teacher?
- Tell me a funny story that happened at school.
- What has been your biggest accomplishment?
- What is the most important thing that's happened to you in your life so far?
- What frustrates you?
- What excites you?
- What inspires you? What are you interested in?
- What makes you happy?
- Tell me about a movie you enjoyed recently. Why did you like it?
- Who was the first girl/boy you liked? What did you like about them?
- Describe your current boyfriend/girlfriend.
- If you could date anyone, who would it be?
- Describe your first job. How much did you make? What were you responsible for?
- How would you describe your parents?
- How would you describe your brothers and sisters?
- How would you describe your grandparents?
- What has been your favorite gift growing up so far?
- What is something you are hoping you will get for your birthday this year?
- If you were being interviewed by a TV station, how would you describe yourself?
- Who are your "best friends?" What are some of your favorite memories with them?
- What sports do you enjoy playing? Which one is your favorite? What are some good stories or fun memories of playing that sport?
- What are your favorite activities or hobbies?

- What kind of music do you enjoy listening to? Who are your favorite artists?
- What is your favorite TV show?
- Have you ever been in trouble? What did you do? What lessons did you learn?
- What is your favorite food? How about your favorite meal? Describe what you eat on a weekly basis.
- What do you want to be when you grow up?
- What scares you about the future?
- What haven't you done that you are excited to do?
- What is the happiest event you can remember?
- What has been your favorite vacation?
- If you could tell your adult self (10 years in the future) one important thing about you, what would it be? (Something you don't ever want to forget.)
- OTHER QUESTIONS TO ASK

_____

_____

_____

_____

_____

_____

Interview with Young Adults: Question List

- Please state your name and how old you are.
- What is your favorite part of your life right now?
- What has happened since you graduated from high school?
- What has been your biggest life lesson after high school? What has been your biggest accomplishment?

- What are you doing in your life right now? What would you like to be doing?
- Describe your living situation. Do you have roommates? What are they like?
- What inspires you right now? Describe all of your personal interests.
- What scares you? What are you fearful of in the future?
- What was the most trouble you ever got into while growing up? What happened? Did everything work out? What did you take away from that experience?
- Describe your current job. What are you responsible for? Are you happy with this job?
- How would you describe yourself to someone who has never met you?
- Who are your "best friends?" What are some of the things you do with them?
- Are you dating anyone right now? Describe who that person is and what you like about them.
- What has been your best dating relationship? Why did you choose that person?
- What has been your biggest takeaway from dating?
- What sports do you enjoy playing? Which one is your favorite? What are some good stories or fun memories of playing that sport?
- What are your favorite activities/hobbies?
- Tell me a secret about yourself.
- What is your most prized possession?
- What kind of music do you enjoy listening to? Who are your favorite artists?
- Tell me about something you are addicted to.
- What is your favorite TV show?
- What question have you never asked your parents that you would love to know the answer to?
- What is your favorite food? How about your favorite meal?

- Do you have any pets? What are their names and what type of animals are they?
- Where do you see yourself in five years?
- What is the happiest event you can remember in your life so far?
- Describe your favorite vacation.
- Before you retire, what would you like to accomplish? What are some of the things you would need to do to make that possible? Is there anything I can do to help make sure your goals and aspirations are accomplished?
- What are some things you never want to lose sight of as you "grow up?"
- What would you like to do or accomplish in the next 10 years? Twenty years?
- If you could ask your grandparents any questions about any topic, what would you want to know?
- Do you have any regrets?
- If you were to go back in time and meet with yourself at the age of 13, what advice would you give yourself?
- Based upon how you were raised, what is one thing you want to pass along to future generations? What is one thing that you want to avoid passing along?
- What lessons have you learned in your lifetime that you would like to pass on to future generations?
- OTHER QUESTIONS TO ASK

_____

_____

_____

_____

_____

_____

CONCLUSION

CONGRATULATIONS ON TAKING THE TIME to learn more about the loved ones you surround yourself with every day as well as those you don't see often. As I mentioned earlier, this is not a book to be used once and then shelved. It is a tool I would suggest you keep in an easy to reach place because you never know when the next opportunity will present itself to have a deeper conversation with your family and friends. The more you use the book, the easier it will be to open up a dialogue with or without these supplied questions. Be curious and continue to go deeper with your questioning. You will be surprised with how many hidden family historical treasures you will discover as you learn about your loved ones.

Please share your stories and share this book with everyone in your life that matters to you. Give them the gift to learn more about their family and friends. Once they start to use the book, future interviews will become easier with them. They may start to ask you questions that you never thought to ask.

Whatever you do, don't stop asking questions. The hard part is now behind you. Once you have conducted your first interview or simply asked a couple of questions out of the book at a family or friend gathering, you now know how easy it really is. If you are like me, you probably also didn't realize how much you didn't know about your loved ones. Now that you know how simple it is to interview your loved ones and how a little book can create a space to have deeper relationships with them, please continue to ask questions so your family and friend stories don't get lost. Our society is filled with distractions and ways to pull our time and focus away from what really matters in our lives - our loved ones. You now have a tool to help bring that focus back where it belongs.

In my last and only interview with my dad, he said one of his many life lessons was "to never take things for granted." Every time I watch that video it reminds me of how fast our loved ones can be taken from us. My wish for everyone who reads this book is that they create more quality, undistracted time with their family and friends and not take the people in their lives for granted. May we all learn, grow and inspire each other to help create family footsteps for the future generations to follow.

ACKNOWLEDGEMENTS

I WOULD LIKE TO THANK the many people who helped encourage and push this project to completion, especially my friends and family. Daren Carollo, my dear friend who has been a huge supporter of this project and who gave me the inspired idea of documenting recipes. Ben Krantz, not only a true friend but also one of the best photographers I have ever met, who spent countless hours with me around a fire pit, keeping our dads' spirits alive. I send a huge thank you to my family, especially my grandparents, for allowing me to conduct the many hours of interviews during our family vacations, gatherings and holidays. And I would be remiss not to extend a special thanks to my wife, Rena Wilson, for the many hours she spent reading (and re-reading!) my book, over and over again, looking for ways to make it better. I am filled with joy and gratitude knowing that I get to share my life with you, Rena. You are my best friend and my biggest cheerleader.

I also offer my deepest gratitude for the coaching and mentorship from John Leonard, the incredible editing skills of Joelle Hann, with whom I was connected through KNLiterary and the final edit clean up(s) from Melissa O'Keefe. Their help really made my ideas and my words come alive.

Lastly, lots of love and thanks to my Dad who served as the true inspiration for what this book has become today. Though we only had one interview together, I am so grateful for the time I was able to spend with him. His love and tireless motivation continue on in me. I love you, Dad!

ABOUT THE AUTHOR

BRANDON A. MUDD IS AN outgoing, fun-loving, glass-half-full motivational speaker, coach, mentor, and sales manager with a memorable laugh and a great love of his family and friends. Interviewing people has come naturally to him since the age of fifteen when he wrote, produced, and starred in a weekly news broadcast at his high school. His natural ability to engage people continued in college, where he had his own college radio program, an  ongoing job as a wedding DJ, and a post-college stint as a stand-up comedian.

Mudd has spent over eleven years in TV and Internet advertising, seven years in radio advertising, and a year in print advertising.

His happy-go-lucky attitude has allowed him to connect with thousands of people from all walks of life in countless situations. He has figured out that if you ask the right questions in a friendly, genuine, fun-filled way at the right time, people will be more than happy to open up and tell their story.

Mudd is close to his family and loves interviewing them. To him, the best way to honor family is to pass along their love, laughter, and support to everyone he comes into contact with. He believes that everyone has a story worth telling, that laughter and love are the cure to all of life's issues and challenges, and that sharing these amazing tales is the greatest gift of all.

Made in the USA
San Bernardino, CA
13 December 2015